Inside the Gate

Carmel Reilly
Jane Wallace-Mitchell

Australia • Brazil • Japan • Korea • Mexico • Singapore • Spain • United Kingdom • United States

Inside the Gate

Fast Forward
Turquoise Level 17

Text: Carmel Reilly
Illustrations: Jane Wallace-Mitchell
Editor: Cameron Macintosh
Design: James Lowe
Series design: James Lowe
Production controller: Seona Galbally
Audio recordings: Juliet Hill, Picture Start
Spoken by: Matthew King and Abbe Holmes
Reprint: Jennifer Foo

ISBN 978 0 17 012624 3
ISBN 978 0 17 012621 2 (set)

Cengage Learning Australia
Level 7, 80 Dorcas Street
South Melbourne, Victoria Australia 3205
Phone: 1300 790 853

Cengage Learning New Zealand
Unit 4B Rosedale Office Park
331 Rosedale Road, Albany, North Shore NZ 0632
Phone: 0508 635 766

For learning solutions, visit cengage.com.au

Printed in Australia by Ligare Pty Ltd
6 7 8 9 10 11 12 21 20 19 18 17

Evaluated in independent research by staff from the Department of Language, Literacy and Arts Education at the University of Melbourne.

Inside the Gate

Carmel Reilly
Jane Wallace-Mitchell

Contents

Chapter 1	**Waiting for Grandma**	4
Chapter 2	**Out of Town**	10
Chapter 3	**Welcome to the Nursery**	14
Chapter 4	**Coming Back**	22

Waiting for Grandma

Today it is dusty outside.
The wind is whipping at the earth and sending clouds of brown dirt all around the town.

I sit here on the doorstep and watch the women come back from work.

Finally, I see Grandma carrying her basket.
She is covered in dust and looks tired, but she smiles when she sees me.
"What are you up to, Kemzie?" she asks.

"Waiting for you!" I say.
"I want you to come
and help me plant trees."

"Trees?" asks Grandma.

I tell Grandma that someone came
to speak to us at school today
about tree planting.
I tell her I want to help out
in the nursery just out of town
where they grow the trees.

"We need the trees to give us wood,
shade and fruit,
and to help keep the Earth well,"
I say quickly.

Grandma laughs,
and puts her basket down.
"You go if you want,
but I have to make dinner," she says.

Running Words 162

For a moment I feel bad.
I shouldn't leave Grandma now.
I should help her chop wood
for the fire and cook the food
she got at the market.

Since Mum and Dad died,
Grandma has been looking after
all our family.
It's hard work for her.

Chapter 2

Out of Town

I look at Grandma,
not sure what to do.

"Go! Go! But come back
with some wood and some fruit,"
she jokes.

"Okay!" I say,
and I turn and run as fast as I can,
out the door
and down the dusty street out of town.

I follow an old track
that leads towards the hills.

Suddenly, in front of me,
I see the nursery.
It is like a sea of green.
There are trees of all kinds,
and a huge vegetable garden.

I step inside the gate.
It is quiet here, safe from the wind,
and it smells so good.

Welcome to the Nursery

A voice says, "Hello.
I saw you at school today, didn't I?"

I whip around to see the person who came to talk to my class.

"Welcome," she says,
and holds out her hand.
"I am Makena."

"I'm Kemzie," I say.

At the back of the nursery,
people are putting small trees
into sacks.
One of them is my friend, Anne.

We help put the trees
on the back of a truck,
ready for Makena to take them
to farms to be planted.
It's hard work,
but it's fun with Anne.
She makes a joke out of everything.

Makena comes with drinks
and bananas for us.
We sit down.

"When I first came here," says Makena,
"there was nothing, just dirt.
We made a dam."
She points past the trees
to what looks like a huge pile of sand.
"There's a lot of water in there now,
to feed the plants.
After that, we made a little nursery
and grew our first trees."

I look around.
It's hard to think that this place
used to be just dirt.

Makena starts speaking again.
"Years ago,
this country was very green.
But people started
chopping down trees
to make way for farms,
and soon it became a dry, dusty place.
People didn't understand then
how much we needed the trees."

Chapter 4

Coming Back

I want to stay longer,
but it is getting late.
"Can we come back?"
I ask Makena.

"Of course!" she says.
"You girls can even have
your own plants to look after.
We will give you a little money
for every tree you can grow
and pass on to a farmer."

I smile,
thinking how much that would
help Grandma.

"This is to say thank you
for your work today,"
says Makena.
She hands us two large bags each.

It is almost dark when I get home.
"Grandma! Look!" I say,
as I rush inside
and open up the bags I have with me.

Grandma stares at me,
and then at the bags,
and she laughs.
"Fruit and wood," she says.
"Just what we need!"